A WEEKEND WITH VELAZQUEZ

A WEEKEND WITH
Velázquez

Text by Florian Rodari

Translated by Ann Keay Beneduce

RIZZOLI
NEW YORK

It's the weekend…yes, and on top of that, there is a festival today in Madrid. It's not easy to find your way in all this commotion, amid horsedrawn carriages from which bunches of grapes are being thrown by young women in wide-skirted dresses and young noblemen who wave their plumed hats. Come, let's get away from these prancing horses, all the people, and this confusion of color and movement. Let us take refuge in the royal palace. This is my domain. These festivals—I am the one who organizes them. And if you should lose sight of me in the crowd, you need only to say that you are the grandchild of the painter Velázquez.

Whew! Well, here we are sheltered from the heat and noise. Now I'll be able to tell you the story of my life. It is true that I am a painter, but I am also a nobleman. This means I don't need to have a workshop, like an ordinary craftsman, or a studio in the city, where I would have to train apprentices. I don't need to look for clients to buy my paintings either; only the king is allowed to order them from me. You see, by good luck, I had hardly arrived in Madrid when King Philip IV, who was

even younger than I was, noticed my work and chose me to be the official portraitist for his family. I have served him in this way for more than thirty years and I am proud of it, for there is no position more noble for a Spaniard than to serve his king. I know King Philip IV very well: I have painted his likeness at least twenty times, at all ages and on every occasion—in formal costume, in hunting clothes, in the midst of his family or as the general leading his army. Because of the hours I have spent studying his face, I have learned to read his inmost thoughts; better than anyone else I understand his desires, his regrets, his noble nature. Over the years, we have become friends, even though my paintbrush has not always been gentle to him. Recently he repaid my efforts by making me a Knight of the Order of Santiago, the highest honor a nobleman can receive in Spain.

This superb tapestry shows the meeting on June 6, 1660, between Louis XIV, the king of France, and Philip IV, who has just offered his daughter Maria Teresa to be the bride of the French monarch. Velázquez prepared the program and the decorations for the sumptuous wedding ceremonies, which lasted for three days. It must be admitted that the French group, be-wigged and be-ribboned, looks a bit silly in contrast to the simple, severe elegance of the Spanish, the uncontested leaders of taste in Europe at that time.

You see, I have an important job at the royal court, one which takes up a good deal of my time. I am a sort of master of ceremonies, and it is my task to organize the official receptions and plan the journeys of Philip IV. I am responsible for decorating the rooms, choosing the furniture, the gold and silver tableware, and the art collection, as well as for preparing the parties he gives in the royal gardens or in the countryside. I must also make arrangements for the guests in the royal box, plan entertainments for the king and for the queen, advise them about their clothing for special occasions, and even watch over the royal princes at their games. In a word, I supervise that complicated thing we call etiquette. The Spanish take this very seriously. This means that everyone knows his or her social position and maintains it, with clockwork precision, by behaving in just the right way and saying just the correct things. I'm going to tell you something, but you must keep it to yourself: the king strongly dislikes all this sort of thing, even though he must accept it with good grace, as part of the difficult job of being the ruling monarch.

Philip has only one wish: to leave the formal ceremonial clothes and stiff manners of the court behind him and to go deer hunting in the mountains with his dogs and his horses. I would even go so far as to say that Philip does not enjoy working hard. He prefers to have a good time, to hunt, to dance, to give extravagant feasts like the one today, and to go to plays at the theater. The affairs of state bore him—royally! And for a long time—too long a time, no doubt—he has entrusted these matters to his not very farsighted ministers. But if he is perhaps a weak king for the politicians and for those who haven't enough to eat, he is an excellent king for artists and for the arts.

Etiquette—that is what obliges the poor princesses to remain standing for hours in these enormous bell-shaped pannier-skirts that sweep everything along as they go—and beneath which six of you and your sisters could hide! And it is etiquette, too, that forces men to wear, even in the worst summer's heat, these starched white collars called "ruffs" in which they can hardly move. Oh! But I don't complain, for it gives me a chance to paint the marvelous details of these amazing clothes, and I must say I have taken full advantage of this. But still! How can one expect people, shackled by so many rules and by their absurd clothing, almost suffocating in their tightly-laced corsets, to still feel like smiling?

Come, follow me through this little hidden doorway; I'm going to show you the palace ballroom before the orchestra and the dancers invade it. Here you will find a collection of portraits of the royal family, as well as paintings that celebrate the might of the Spanish armies. Here (above) is Philip IV, well-seated on his rearing horse—notice his air of calm assurance and how he seems to dominate the landscape that stretches out beneath his feet. Ah! if only he were always so self-assured in his daily decisions as the chief-of-state!

Facing him is Elizabeth, the charming daughter of Henry IV of France and Maria de Medici; she was married to Philip IV when she was only thirteen years old. She is shown on her favorite horse, dressed in a doublet and skirt of extravagant richness. But look carefully at this painting, which I had begun work on before leaving on a trip to Italy. While I was away, Elizabeth's dress and the tapestry horse-blanket on which she is seated were decorated by one of my assistants, a good artist, fanatically meticulous, but rather boring, as he repeated the same pattern over and over, without feeling.

When I got back from my trip, I took up work on the painting, but only did the horse's head and the landscape that lies behind the subject. But here is where you can see my "hand," that is, the special way in which I apply the oil paints to the canvas with my brush; my touch is quick, fluent, almost careless-looking, seemingly imprecise. The reason I use these transparent, wavering, almost blurry strokes is that, when you look at the picture from a little distance, they give a feeling of life, of the air vibrating around an object, like the fluffy mane of the horse, or the wind-tossed landscape. I may use this technique to give the out-of-focus effect of things seen at a distance, like these people standing on a balcony. Sometimes, to emphasize the impression of liveliness and impatience, I may even repeat a detail, almost without meaning to; you can see it here, in the way I have painted the horse's left front hoof.

The jewel the queen is wearing is an enormous pearl that was found inside an oyster so small it was nearly thrown back into the sea. This jewel is called "La Peregrina"—The Wanderer— because it has traveled so much. Recently it was owned by the actress Elizabeth Taylor.

In the center, between the portraits of his parents and over the door through which the crowds of courtiers will soon be entering, is a painting of Prince Baltasar Carlos, heir to the throne, who died, alas, much too soon. Of all of the king's children, he is the one I always liked the best. He had a proud, serious manner that gave the impression that he would be able to restore Spain's former glory and its pleasant way of life. I've shown him here in his uniform as a little general, holding the staff of command and wearing across his chest the crimson sash that denotes the highest military rank. Baltasar Carlos learned to ride horseback in his earliest childhood and does it astonishingly well. I have painted another portrait of him (opposite) showing him having one of his first riding lessons, supervised by the prime minister, the Duke of Olivares. On the balcony one can barely make out, in the warm light of a late afternoon in summer, the king and queen, who are watching the scene, surrounded by their courtiers. Behind the horse you can also see that rascal, Juan de Lazcano, one of those dwarfs I will tell you about later. . .

Now I'm going to show you the biggest picture I have painted in my whole career. Ah, but it's true, you are too small to see it from there. Wait, take off your shoes and climb up on the king's throne. No, don't be afraid, he won't scold you—it would probably even make him laugh to see you there. Now can you see it better? Doesn't it have a lot of people in it? Since I didn't have room to show all of the soldiers who came with the two generals, I decided to suggest their presence by a forest of lances which you can see sticking up at the right of the picture. That is why this painting is sometimes called "Las Lanzas" (The Lances). The exact event that I have chosen to recreate here with my paintbrushes is one that took place on June 2, 1625. On that date the defeated Dutch general, Justin of Nassau, was obliged to hand to his victor, General Spinola, chief of the Spanish army, the key to the city of Breda, of which, until now, he had been the protector. You can imagine what a painful ceremony this was for the conquered general and his troops.

The little Dutch city of Breda, which can be seen in the background, had at that time been fighting for its independence from Spanish rule.

But even though he is a soldier through and through as well as a conqueror, a nobleman always respects his enemy. I have tried to suggest this chivalrous sentiment in this painting, showing as naturally as possible the gestures and facial expressions of the people meeting here. As a sign of his surrender, the defeated Dutchman at left is just about to kneel and hand the key to the city to the Spanish general, but Spinola is reaching over to hold him back, to spare him from this added humiliation. Placing his hand almost affectionately on the Dutchman's shoulder, he seems to be saying, with a courteous smile, "No, my friend, your defeat is bitter enough. I don't want to make it harsher by asking you to bow down at my feet. Get up, I beg you." This is, you see, a fine example of chivalrous behavior—a part of the etiquette I was telling you about a little while ago—it tells us we should always respect other people, especially if they are in some kind of sorrow, and we must be courteous at all times.

Look out, here they come! Listen to their shouts and laughter. Watch out for all this uproar and confusion! Come, let's go up this circular staircase and slip away. I don't want to meet them today and hear them say, "Senor Velázquez, por favor, don Diego, oiga." Some days I feel like leaving all this turmoil and retiring to the country, where I could live peacefully with you, far away from these constant celebrations and endless receptions.

"Por favor" means "please" and "oiga" means "listen" in Spanish.

Wait a minute, let's sit on this bench, I'm going to tell you about the great favor the king granted me a few years ago. Having decided to remodel his palace, which had become too small for the entire royal court to live in, he sent me to Italy to buy works of art for it: sculptures, decorative objects, and paintings. You can imagine he didn't have to ask me twice! As soon as my bags were packed, I went first to Venice and then to Rome. It was in that unforgettable city that I was happier than I had ever been in my life, so much so that the king had to write several stern letters urging me to return to his court. For there, in Rome, I didn't have to worry about palace matters. I was free to wander about the streets and gardens of the city and to make trips to the surrounding countryside. I was totally charmed by the Italian way of life, so much gayer and more carefree than ours. . .

Throughout the ages, painters have adored Rome, its light, its harmonious surroundings, the sweetness of life there. The great French painter Jean-Dominique Ingres (1780–1867) stayed there even longer than Velázquez and made a number of sketches of it, like this view of Castle Gondolfo, near Lake d'Albano.

One day an important official of the church asked me to paint a portrait of the pope, who lived in the Vatican palace. I hesitated at first, as I had not touched my paintbrushes in a long time, but after a few practice sketches I made up my mind to do it. Then I met with Pope Innocent X who, because of his innumerable appointments could only pose for me for about an hour. I locked myself in my studio after this, and a few days later I delivered the portrait. I was afraid that I would be thrown into prison, for I knew that the portrait I had done of the pope was not at all flattering. On my canvas the head of the church—with his stern expression, his huge nose, his thick lips—did not have the air of an angelic choirboy. . . But the sovereign pontiff who, beneath his strong, almost fierce appearance was really a man of intelligence and good will, had the good grace to say that it was a good likeness—perhaps even too good a likeness! The portrait was shown to the public and, if I do say so myself, was greatly admired and often copied.

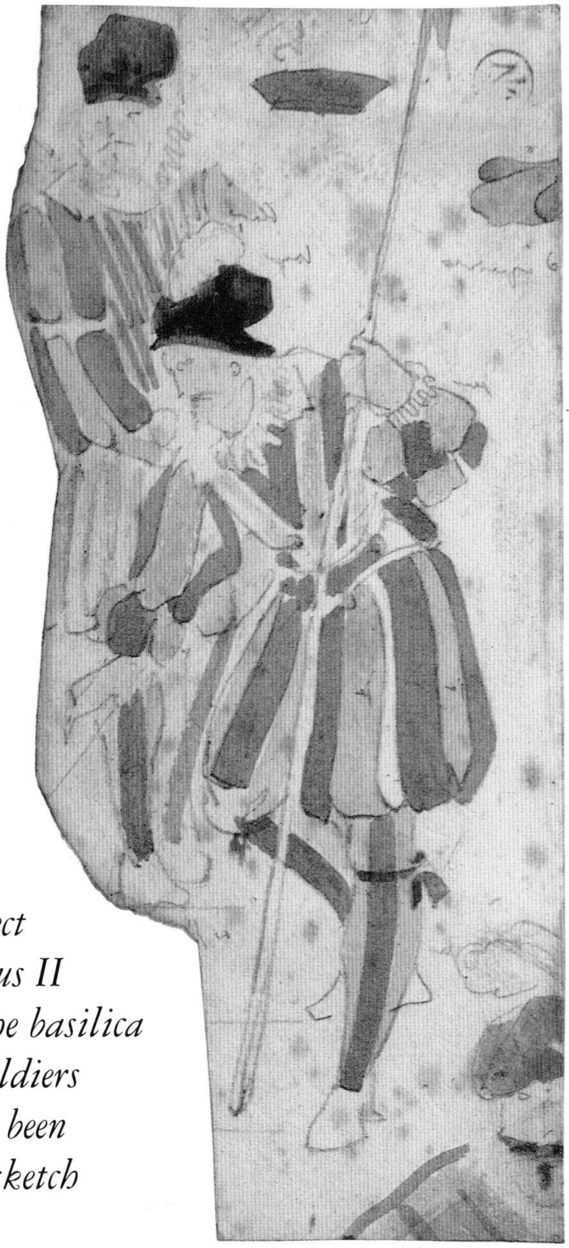

The company of the Swiss Guards, who protect Rome's Vatican City, was created by Pope Julius II in 1506, the same year in which he founded the basilica of St. Peter. The striking uniforms of the footsoldiers were designed by Michelangelo, and have often been drawn by other artists, such as Ingres in the sketch at right.

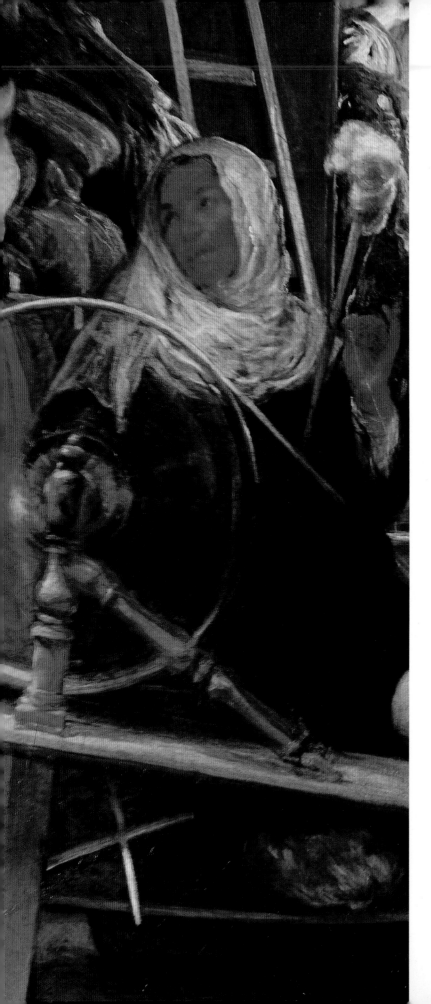

But, you see, I don't take a lot of credit for that, for, even though I go to great pains to render my sitters faithfully, I have no imagination at all; I can only paint what I see. To be like a poet in paint, telling stories and daydreams of strange animals and little angels, or to experiment with the effects of colors not found in nature—I cannot do such things. And when, one day, I tried to do a painting that told an ancient Greek legend—the story of a young woman who challenged a goddess at the art of weaving and was punished by being turned into a spider—well, no one understood it. I had, in effect, placed ghost-like figures of the gods and goddesses all the way in the back of the painting, where they appeared to be mere figures in a tapestry!

On the other hand, I had given all the importance to the everyday people, workers and servants. I did the same in another picture of a blacksmith and his helpers, people I had seen in their workshops with my own eyes. Being unable to conjure up fairies or make up stories, I came back to pure and simple description of what was familiar to me. Hands, for instance—do you know why I give such importance to hands in my paintings? From their positions, their ways of grasping things, sometimes delicately, sometimes firmly, you can almost tell what is going through the heads of the people they belong to. I take care to show how objects and materials really look and feel—and even to show how things look in motion, like this spinning-wheel (opposite) turning at full speed.

There are, however, many painters who lived not so long ago and whom I admire, painters like Titian and El Greco, who seemed to paint in a waking dream, working from their imaginations. Even a simple landscape seemed to become an opportunity for them to suggest another world. I once saw an extraordinary painting by El Greco, called *A View of Toledo,* the city where he lived. But it was not a painting of a real place, where you could walk on the real earth; the painter had forced and deepened the colors until they seemed phantasmagorical. He had exaggerated the shapes of the clouds, the buildings, and the mountains so that in looking at this painting one got the impression that a thunderstorm was about to break forth, or that something dramatic was on the verge of happening, or maybe that the heavens were about to open and hurl God's angry thunderbolt down to strike the earth and split it in two! To put it briefly, he painted all the kinds of things that are in the restless souls of men but which one never sees in real life.

But for me, a landscape is simply something like this—a corner of a garden with an old wooden building, a cloth draped on the balustrade—nothing divine, nothing you could not touch, nothing you could not come back to find again tomorrow, just the way you left it.

In the eyes of someone like me who has chosen the work of seeing and making seen, all things visible on this earth are of equal value: an old crust of stale bread can keep me busy as long as, or even longer than the pearl that hangs from the ear of a princess. Just because we live today in a palace, among kings and their celebrations, doesn't mean that we should forget all those who live in the shadows and who have very little. When I lived in Seville I painted some of the nameless, penniless people I met on every streetcorner. Without meaning to, just because their natural dignity captured my attention, I made nobles of them! The water-carrier who gives you a glass of water, cool and sweet-smelling, when you are overcome by the furnace-like heat of a summer's day—isn't he more generous than the most powerful ruler on earth? And could one enjoy a better feast when one is hungry than three fresh eggs fried in a clay pot? So why should I paint a torn cloak, an apron, a pot-bellied jug, or some onion peelings with less care than the silks and velvets worn by princesses, or their beautiful golden hair?

If one can find in every man a king, it is also true that behind every king hides an ordinary man. So that the powerful people of this world will never forget that, in spite of the pomp of their ceremonies and the authority of their positions, misery, poverty, ugliness, and illness are always present, the court of Spain is surrounded by people who serve as constant reminders of this truth—dwarfs, jesters, and simpletons. There are many of these "people of pleasure" (as they cruelly call them here) in the palace. On one hand, their physical or mental handicaps emphasize by contrast the beauty or intelligence of those who have such gifts; on the other hand, they bring back to earth those who have a tendency to wander among the clouds and fancy they look like gods. And, if the dwarfs at the court of Philip IV are deprived of normal height or of clear minds, they have, in compensation, the right to be rude, to dress as they please, and to say out loud whatever they think, even to the king. Their shouts and jokes fill the corridors with bursts of laughter, and their witty remarks, always barbed, amuse the courtiers, who then get even by meddling in their affairs.

Velázquez was not the only one in his time to paint dwarfs and deformed people. Look at these two portraits at the left, and compare them with those by lesser-known painters (shown, smaller, also at left). Velázquez knew how to portray the handicaps of his models without making them look grotesque.

Animals, too, have their dignity. I remember a magnificent stag that the king chased for several days without capturing it. When he finally caught him in his cloth-walled trap, Philip set the stag free again because he recognized in him his equal: a real king of the forest, unconquered, fearless, proud, and serene. And I painted his portrait, as I had so often painted Philip's.

Hunting is the favorite diversion of the king of Spain. He is tireless, spending days and days chasing every kind of game in the forests surrounding Madrid. A stag is hunted in a special ceremony reserved for members of the royal court. Driven from cover by the hounds, followed for a long time, the animal is finally chased into a long corridor of walls made of cloth hanging down to the ground. There the king and noblemen of Spain await it, to stab it to death with knives, under the impassive gaze of the women of the court.

Good heavens! Here comes that tiresome
marquis of Malpica and his tall beanpole of a
daughter! Will we never find any peace? Let's
go through this gallery that leads to my
studio. There, at least, no one will disturb us,
and you will see my latest painting—I've just
finished it. I'm curious to know what you'll
think of it. But let's stop here for a minute. I
love to stroll and think in these corridors.
Have you noticed the mirrors all along the
walls? The tall windows and the doors that
open on countless rooms? Can you imagine
the games you could play here with all these

looking-glasses? The space seems much
bigger than it is because of their reflections,
and the many openings make it even more
complicated. People and furniture seem to be
constantly caught in a sort of trap or puzzle.
Look carefully—if you place yourself between
two mirrors you will see yourself reflected to
infinity, and when you think you are going
away in one direction, your double goes off
the other way. It's magic, don't you agree? I
love mirrors. I've used them more than once
in paintings, to trick people. . .

This detail of The Painter's Family, *a painting by his son-in-law, shows us Velázquez working on a portrait of an* infanta. *That is what they call a princess in Spain. The infantas were waited on by the young daughters of noble families, who were called* meninas.

Ah! Here we are. No one around? All the better. One can't say that I haven't enough room, don't you agree? My studio is in the room that used to be occupied by the prince Baltasar Carlos. Here is the painting I was just telling you about. I named it *The Royal Family,* but it is universally known as *Las Meninas.* So far, no one has realized that behind this group portrait, which seems to be perfectly straightforward at first sight, a big secret is hidden. Let's look at it together. Right away, you will recognize me, at the left, holding my paintbrush in one hand and my palette in the other. I've taken a few steps backward to get away from the large canvas I am working on, and I am looking straight ahead.

A little more to the front, in the light that comes from a high window on the right and which floods the whole foreground, are five figures. There is the menina Doña Maria Agustino Sarmiento, kneeling and offering a pot of hot chocolate to the Infanta Margarita. Margarita is the enchanting daughter of Philip IV and his young queen. Then there is another maid of honor, the menina Doña Isabel de Velasco, who bows her head slightly in the direction of her little mistress without taking her eyes away from whatever fascinating scene she is really watching. At her right the dwarf Mari-Barbola seems immobilized by what she sees, while the charming little dwarf Nicolasito Pertusato daringly puts his foot on a drowsy mastiff.

In the shadow behind the group of children you can distinguish two more people: these are two court officials, very bored, who must watch over the little world of the royal children. Finally, far at the back of the room, in the light of the open doorway, you can see the dark figure of Don José Nieto Velázquez, a distant cousin of mine, who has a job somewhat like my own here at the court. But what is it that everyone is looking at so persistently? It seems as if almost everyone is looking at the same thing. You can't guess what it is? Look carefully at all parts of the painting. What do you see on the back wall, to the left of the doorway? Do you see two heads, strangely lighted, inside a frame? Yes, you are right, that is not a painting—it's a mirror, a mirror that reflects the images . . . of the king and queen. *Now* do you understand the secret?

Actually, I am busy painting the royal couple who pose for me under the watchful eyes of the infanta and her meninas!

By showing the royal couple in the hazy distance of the mirror, Velázquez could hide the age difference between the king and the queen, Marianne of Austria, who was thirty years younger than her husband.

And now let me tell you what just happened. A few seconds ago, the pretty little infanta came into the room with Don José Nieto, who is now leaving. The two meninas immediately ran to the little infanta to greet her. But she does not bother with them—she is looking at her parents, feeling a little shy, and yet quite sure that they'll be pleased to see her as she knows she looks very pretty in her new, full-skirted gown. And, indeed, finding her little daughter so charming, her mother blushes with pleasure. You can see her rosy cheeks reflected palely in the mirror. But, you may ask, why can't one see the royal couple themselves? Is it because they are standing in exactly the same place as you, the viewer? No, it is even more subtle than that, you see! Look how this scene is set within the space. You—or the viewer, if you prefer—are really placed *behind* the king and queen, in the doorway that leads to my studio, facing the door in the background of the painting. We can't quite see the royal couple because there is a wall that hides them from us. They, however, are *in* the room, just to the left, between us and the group of children. We were passing by chance, unexpectedly, and have come upon this charming scene of an adorable princess who has just arrived and interrupted the sitting. It is the startled face of Mari-Barbola who betrays our presence and makes us enter the picture, too.

So that's my big secret. By placing myself inside the picture I was painting, I was able to bring in three more people, three invisible people: the king, the queen, and you, the viewer. Thus I have made you pass through to the other side of the "looking-glass." Or, if you like, I've made the persons inside the painting step out of the picture and bring their world to join our own. Now that you know this, you can just step through the frame of the door—or the frame of the painting, it's all the same—and go greet this noble gathering. Go ahead, be brave, go make a nice bow, and don't be afraid of the dog, he loves children. . .

WHERE TO SEE VELAZQUEZ

There aren't too many examples of Velázquez's work in the United States, but here are a few museums where you can find them:

New York, New York

The wonderful Metropolitan Museum of Art has one of the biggest collections of art treasures in the world. To see everything in their collection would take you many weeks or months of study. The museum has four paintings by Velázquez, but they are not always on exhibition. If you go to the rooms where they display European paintings, you may be lucky enough to see a portrait of Juan de Pareja, Don Gaspar de Guzmán (Count-Duke Olivares), or of the Infanta Maria Teresa of Spain.

If you walk along Fifth Avenue you will come to The Frick Collection which was once the private home of Henry Clay Frick. You will find a portrait of King Philip IV among the many other European masterpieces here.

Boston, Massachusetts

In this city you will find quite a few paintings by Velázquez, and some he did with the help of the painter's who worked in his workshop. In the Museum of Fine Arts you will see several portraits of people at the Spanish court; King Philip IV, the Infanta Maria Teresa, and Don Baltasar Carlos and a dwarf. At the Isabella Stewart Gardner Museum there is a portrait of Prince Philip, and for something different go across the Charles River to the Harvard University campus, and see the *Portrait of an Elderly Man* at the Fogg Art Museum.

Washington D.C.

At the National Gallery of Art you will find *The Needlewoman*, a portrait of a young man (actually done by students of Velázquez), and, best of all, a study he did for the famous portrait of Pope Innocent X.

Cleveland, Ohio

The Cleveland Museum of Art has a *Portrait of the Jester Calabazas*, who lived at the court in Velázquez's time.

If you really want to "enter" the world that Velázquez painted, there is just one thing to do—ask your parents to take you to Madrid, to the Prado Museum. More than half of our painter's works—including some of his most important paintings—can be found there. But let us hope you won't have to wait in line, as was the case in 1990 when there was a big exhibition of his works, and some of his admirers had to wait more than four hours just to get into the first room.

Other museums in Europe where you can see his work are the Kunsthistorisches Museum in Vienna and the National Gallery and the Wallace Collection in London. There are not very many of his paintings in France except at the Louvre Museum in Paris and at the Beaux Arts Museums in Orléans and in Rouen. In Orléans there is the magnificent painting of *St. Thomas*, and in Rouen you can see the remarkable portrait of *A Geographer*.

VELAZQUEZ IN HISTORY

Velázquez was born in 1599 in one of the prettiest and liveliest cities of the time: the Andalusian city of Seville, on the banks of the Guadalquivir River. Seville was a wealthy city due to the immense treasures of gold and silver brought back from the Americas in Spanish galleons which had to pass through this port. In its markets one could find things from all over the world. Its inhabitants were very cultivated, its women noted for their beauty. In spite of the tropical heat, life was very pleasant in the palaces with their shady gardens. The distinctive architecture of Seville mingled European Renaissance style with Moorish and Arabic traditions rooted in the eighth century. The city attracted many artists and excellent scholars, so it is not surprising that Velázquez received a very good education, not only in painting but also in many other subjects: geography, astronomy, medicine, mechanics, and even horseback riding. Very soon Velázquez was considered the best painter in Seville, but because he was also a very ambitious young man, he decided to go to Madrid. This was the city where the young king of Spain, Philip IV, who had ascended the throne in 1621, now lived, surrounded by his court. On Velázquez's first trip there in 1622, the king was too busy to pose for him; however, the next year, recommended by his compatriot the Count-Duke of Olivares who had become prime minister, Velázquez was finally more successful and was able to paint a large full-length standing portrait of the nineteen-year-old Philip IV. This first royal commission, very well received, opened the palace doors to the young man from Seville, both as a painter and as a member of the court. Over the next forty years, he painted the king and other members of the royal family many times and received many of the country's most distinguished honors for his work.

In taking the throne, Philip IV inherited an immense kingdom acquired over the course of the sixteenth century by his Roman Catholic forebears, Charles V and then Philip II and Isabella, a kingdom whose unity was now threatened by both external and internal revolts and crises. Abroad, the United Provinces of the Netherlands, were the first to rise up against Spanish rule (1648), then its other possessions in Italy and Flanders also freed themselves. On the Iberian peninsula, Portugal won its independence in 1640, followed a few years later by Catalonia. And with neighboring France, despite mutual respect and many marriages between the two royal families, relationships had been deteriorating throughout the century, until the Peace of the Pyrenees, signed in 1659, sealed the supremacy of France. Spain became isolated; not only did the Spanish government not seem to know how to deal with growing economic problems and the gradual loss of the American markets on which their prosperity was built, but the Church drove the Moors and Protestants, who had formerly stimulated foreign trade, from the country. The inactivity of the nobility, who disdained work, the corruption that pervaded every level of society and, in addition, repeated outbreaks of the plague, all precipitated the decline of Spain's political and military power.

The king was in large part responsible for this situation. His weakness of character, his distaste for politics and his lack of self-discipline led him to all sorts of wrong decisions and shameful compromises. His weakness worked to the benefit of Olivares, the prime minister, a man who, contrary to the king, was energetic, hardworking, and intelligent and who soon had a very strong influence over his ruler. Depending on his ministers in all things, Philip IV felt free to give himself over to a life of pleasure, devoted to women, the hunt, and extravagant celebrations. The extraordinary expenses for these royal diversions emptied the country's treasuries. After the disgrace and dismissal of Olivares in 1643, the king tried to mend his ways and take up the reins of power. But despite a few military successes which gave some small hope to the Spanish, the end of Philip IV's reign was a series of failures and sorrows. He lost his wife to whom he was very much attached, and the next year he learned of the death of his sister Maria. Then, and worst of all, his beloved son Baltasar Carlos, the heir to the throne for whom everyone had high hopes, died of malaria. Everything had collapsed. Neither his subsequent marriage to his niece Marianne of Austria, nor the birth of his daughter Margarita, whose radiant beauty is depicted in *Las Meninas,* could dissipate the deep depression that, in his later years, made the king very suspicious and irritable. So much so, in fact, that when he died in 1665, five years after the death of his favorite painter, there were few to weep for him.

But even though Spain, the land of Cervantes, had lost its position on the political and economic maps, and seemed unable to adjust to the advent of great changes in the world, it still remained a model in the fields of manners and culture. And although he was blamed by his people for being a weak ruler, Philip IV knew well how to have a good time and gave the Spanish court spectacles and entertainments that made the rest of Europe pale with envy. It was not just painting that he loved; he had an equal passion for the theater and commissioned many impressive plays from dramatists of the period: Calderón de la Barca, Lope de Vega, Tirso de Molina, and Francisco Quevedo. Performances took place on the innumerable anniversaries that marked the Spanish calendar, secular or religious holidays, among which the Carnival was by far the most popular, mixing as it does, for several days each year, people from all levels of society. The king also loved embellishing his palaces, building new hunting pavilions, or having sumptuous gardens designed for his extravagant parties—gardens on which architects, gardeners, decorators, and fountain-builders lavished all their knowledge and ingenuity. Velázquez was in charge of many of these creations and was very good at preparing them; no doubt a great deal of his work, now lost, consisted of decorative canvases hastily painted as settings for these ephemeral events.

The court of Madrid was a city in itself, with thousands of residents, servants and courtiers, who had to be lodged, fed and cared for. Diego Rodríguez de Silva y Velázquez (the names of his father and mother) occupied a privileged rank among them, and lived in the palace with his family. Thanks to the king's friendship, he was able to travel twice to Italy, in 1629 and again in 1649–50. These were the only two vacations in the painter's life. Philip IV protected him, trusted him with important tasks, and favored him with admission to the Order of the Knights of Santiago, an honor reserved for the most noble families. The painter often accompanied the king on his travels and it was on his return from one such trip, to Fuenterrabia, where he had gone to decorate and furnish the royal palace in preparation for the wedding of the Infanta Maria-Teresa and her fiancé King Louis XIV of France, that he fell ill. He died a few days later, on August 6, 1660.

Atlantic Ocean

FRANCE

Oviedo

Santiago de
Compostela

Fuenterrabia

ASTURIAS

BASQUE
TERRITORY

GALICIA

NAVARRO

Pyrenees

LEON

Valladolid

Ebro

CATALONIA

OLD
CASTILE

Salamanca

Barcelona

Segovia

ARAGON

■ THE ESCORIAL PALACE

PORTUGAL

Madrid

Tajo

VALENCIA

Valencia
(the city)

Balearic Islands

NEW
CASTILE

ESTREMADURA

MURCIA

Mediterranean Sea

Cordoba

Seville

Guadalquivir

Granada

ANDALUSIA

Cadiz

Málaga

Strait of Gibraltar

Atlantic Ocean

VELAZQUEZ'S SPAIN

Velázquez was born in June of 1599 in Seville. He died on
August 6, 1660 in Madrid. Among the great European artists
who lived at about the same time as Velázquez are: El Greco,
Zurbarán, and Murillo (Spain): Louis Le Nain, Georges de La
Tour, and Nicolas Poussin (France); Bernini (Italy); Rubens and
Van Dyck (Flanders); Rembrandt and Vermeer (The Netherlands).

IMPORTANT DATES IN THE
LIFE OF VELÁZQUEZ

1599   Diego Rodríguez de Silva y Velázquez is born in Seville to Juan Rodríguez de Silva and Jerónima Velázquez. In signing his paintings, the painter always used his mother's surname.

1610–
1617   Velázquez is apprenticed to Francisco Pacheco, a painter and art historian in Seville. After seven years Velázquez qualifies as a master and enters the painter's guild, which gives him the right to practice his art anywhere in Spain.

1618   The painter marries Juana de Miranda Pacheco, the daughter of his master, on April 23rd in Seville.

1619   Francisca, Velázquez's first daughter, is born.

1622–
1623   Velázquez visits Madrid twice. The second time he is invited back by the Count-Duke of Olivares and is asked to paint Philip IV's portrait. He is appointed painter to the king during this visit and moves to Madrid with his family.

1624–
1628   His portraits of King Philip the IV, the Count-Duke of Olivares and other courtiers earn him great praise and the title of Gentleman Usher.

1629–
1630   Velázquez receives permission from the king to visit Italy. He goes to Genoa, Milan, Venice, Bologna, and Rome, where he spends a year. He returns to Madrid in January 1631.

1634–
1635   He paints *Las Lanzas* (The Lances).

1646   He receives the new title of Gentleman of the Bedchamber and is called upon to play an important part in official ceremonies.

1648   Velázquez's yearly pension is increased to 700 ducats. He is a member of the Spanish delegation sent to Trent to bring back the king's new bride, Archduchess Marianne of Austria.

1649–
1651   The artist travels to Italy and purchases paintings by Titian, Tintoretto, and Veronese for the royal collections. His travels lead to a long stay in Rome where he paints the portrait of Pope Innocent X.

1652   He is appointed to the high position of Marshal of the Royal Household by the king.

1656–
1660   Velázquez paints *Las Meninas* (The Maids of Honor), his most famous painting, and his last great work *Las Hilanderas* (The Tapestry Weavers, or The Fable of Arachne).

1658   Philip IV appoints Velázquez to the Order of Santiago, an honor that recognizes his nobility and his contributions to the court.

1660   In April, Velázquez leaves Madrid for Fuenterrabia in northern Spain to decorate the royal residence of the king's daughter Maria Teresa and King Louis XIV of France. After returning to Madrid in June, he becomes ill and dies.

LIST OF ILLUSTRATIONS

Page 15

Equestrian Portrait of Elizabeth of France (wife of Philip IV), c. 1635 (301 x 314 cm.), London, collection of the Duke of Westminster.

Page 16

The Riding Lesson, detail, Madrid, Prado.

La Peregrina, pearl belonging to the royal family, purchased by Elizabeth Taylor in 1969.

Page 17

Equestrian Portrait of Elizabeth of France, detail, Madrid, Prado.

Page 18

Prince Don Baltasar Carlos on Horseback, c. 1635 (209 x 123 cm.), Madrid, Prado.

Page 19

The Riding Lesson, entire and detail, c. 1635 (144 x 96.5 cm.), London, collection of the Duke of Westminster.

Pages 20–21

The Surrender of Breda, or *The Lances*, 1634–1635 (307 x 367 cm.), Madrid, Prado.

Page 22

The Surrender of Breda, detail, Madrid, Prado.

Page 23

Bramante (1444–1514): Spiral staircase of the Belvedere, Rome, Vatican Museum.

Pages 24–25

Jean-Dominique Ingres (1780–1867): *View of Gandolfo Castle near Lake d'Albano*, lead pencil and watercolor (45 x 81 cm.), Montauban, Ingres Museum.

Page 26

Portrait of Pope Innocent X, 1650 (140 x 120 cm.), Rome, Doria Pamphili Gallery.

Pages 28–29

The Weavers or *The Legend of Arachne*, c. 1657 (220 x 289 cm.), Madrid, Prado.

Page 30

The Weavers, detail, Madrid, Prado.

Page 31
Apollo in Vulcan's Forge, 1630, detail, Madrid, Prado.

Page 32
El Greco (1541–1614): *View of Toledo*, between 1595 and 1610, (121 x 129 cm.), New York, Metropolitan Museum of Art.

Page 33
View of the Garden of the Villa Medici in Rome, c. 1650 (48 x 52 cm.), Madrid, Prado.

Page 34
The Watercarrier of Seville, c. 1620 (106 x 82 cm.), London, Wellington Museum.

Page 35
An Old Woman Cooking Eggs, entire and details, 1618 (99 x 128 cm.), Edinburgh, National Gallery of Scotland.

Page 36
Top: *Portrait of the Court Dwarf Sebastián de Morra*, c. 1644 (107 x 82 cm.), Madrid, Prado.

Bottom: *Portrait of the Court Dwarf Don Diego de Acedo "El Primo,"* 1644 (107 x 82 cm.), Madrid, Prado.

Juan Carreño de Miranda (1614–1685): *The Monstrosity,* dressed and nude, c. 1640 (165 x 107 cm.), Madrid, Prado.

Page 37
Juan Van der Hamen y León (1596–1631): *Dwarf*, c. 1626 (122 x 67 cm.), Madrid, Prado.

Page 38
Head of a Stag, c. 1634 (66 x 52 cm.), Madrid, Prado.

Page 39
Juan Bautista Martínez del Mazo (1612–1667): *The Deer Hunt at Aranjuez*, c. 1626 (122 x 87 cm.), Madrid, Prado.

Page 40–41
Hall of mirrors, Rome, Doria Pamphili Gallery.

Page 42

Juan Bautista Martínez del Mazo: *The Painter's Family*, detail, c. 1650, Vienna, Kunsthistorisches Museum.

Pages 43–47, 49

Las Meninas, 1656 (318 x 276 cm.), entire and details, Madrid, Prado.
Model based on *Las Meninas* by Pierre-Marie Valat and Pierre Pitrou, Paris.

Pages 50–51:

Lines of visitors at the entrance to the Prado Museum during the Velázquez exhibition in 1990.

Page 51

Top: *St. Thomas*, c. 1620 (94 x 73 cm.), Orleans, Musée des Beaux-Arts.

Bottom: *The Geographer*, c. 1627 (98 x 81 cm.), Rouen, Musée des Beaux-Arts.

Page 52

Matthäus Merian (1593–1650): *View of Seville*, etching.

Other books in the Weekend with Series

Leonardo da Vinci
Rembrandt
Degas
Renoir
Picasso

First published in the United States of America in 1993 by
Rizzoli International Publications, Inc.
300 Park Avenue South, New York, New York 10010

Series under the direction of R. Skira and Y.-M. Maquet
Copyright © 1992 by Editions d'Art Albert Skira S. A., Geneva
English edition copyright © 1993 by Rizzoli International Publications, Inc.

Library of Congress Cataloging-in-Publication Data

Rodari, Florian.
    [Dimanche avec Velázquez. English]
    A weekend with Velázquez / text by Florian Rodari ; English translation
by Ann Keay Beneduce.
        p. cm.
    Summary: The seventeenth-century Spanish artist discusses his life and
    paintings.
    ISBN 0-8478-1647-8
    1. Velásquez, Diego, 1599–1660—Juvenile literature. 2. Painters—
Spain—Biography—Juvenile literature. [1. Velásquez, Diego, 1599–1660.
2. Artists.] I. Title.
ND813.V4R62 1993
759.6—dc20   92-33350
                                                                    CIP
                                                                     AC

Photography credits:
Archivo Oronoz, Madrid, pp. 4–5; L.A.R.A., Madrid (Photo J. Martín), pp. 6,
9, 12, 13, 14, 15, 16, 17, 18, 19, 20–21, 22, 28–29, 30, 31, 33, 34, 36, 39,
43–49; Collection du Mobilier National, Paris, p. 10; Christie's New York
(Silver Department), p. 11 (2 ill.); © Sotheby's, p. 16; Montauban,
Roumagnac Photographe, pp. 24–25, 27; Archivo iconografico S.A. (AISA)
Madrid, p. 36; Photo ARRIS & Co., Rome, pp. 40–41; Photo Meyer, Vienna,
p. 42; © Europa Press, pp. 50–51.

The analysis of Las Meninas was based on a research paper by Dr. Bartolomé
Mestré Fiol, published in the magazine *Mayurca,* Number 8, Palma de
Mallorca, 1972.

Design by Mary McBride

Printed in Hong Kong